YOUR DECLUTTER CHALLENGE

The Best Guide to Organizing Your Home in 30 Easy Steps

The Path to the New You

We're Gunna Kick Your Clutter to the Curb, *Literally!*

Your home is your oasis. It's meant to be an escape from the work and stress of the outside world, not a chaotic place where you simply store your stuff.

If you walk through your front door and are greeted by piles of papers, laundry, and dishes, you may start to *dread* coming home in the first place. Maybe every surface in your home seems to be piled with "stuff" or you're constantly misplacing things, like the bills that need to be paid. If you struggle to find a clear spot on your countertop to make dinner or you have to step on dirty clothes and wet towels on your bathroom floor, your home could be making you feel unhappy and overwhelmed.

Every single thing you own is one more thing you have to think about and take care of. The stress and pressure of keeping up with your physical belongings can really take a toll on your happiness and your health.

If you're feeling resentful for having to constantly clean, tidy, and maintain the stuff in your house, you're not alone. Thankfully, your home doesn't have to be just another chore on your never-ending to-do list. Your home can really be the beautiful, relaxing space you and your family deserve.

But How Do You Create a Home That Makes You Feel Calm and Happy Instead of Super Stressed and

a Little Ragey?

One word: declutter.

You can buy dozens of storage bins and make all the to-do lists you want, but if you don't understand *why* you are cluttered and take the right steps to declutter properly, you'll never be able to stop the cycle of clutter for good. Decluttering means less stuff to clean and keep track of and more space in your home for actual living.

And it's more than just getting rid of your things. It's a shift in your mindset from always thinking about the past and worrying about the future to fully embracing the present. Decluttering your physical space declutters your mind. Your home is the foundation for your entire life and, when it's cluttered and messy, your day-to-day life can feel cluttered and messy too.

Every single person living in your home is negatively affected by clutter. The chaos can make it difficult to relax at bedtime or may leave you and your family feeling angry, frustrated, or depressed, without even knowing why. When your physical environment is clean and calm, you can't help but feel more in control of your mental and emotional environment too.

Decluttering will impact every area of your life. Less stuff means more time, more money, more motivation, and...the best part? More happiness.

Ready? Let's declutter all the things!

Your Decluttering Plan Is Right Here

This journal will guide you toward making those positive, real life changes. In its pages, you'll find a complete roadmap to a clutter-free home in thirty easy steps.

Some steps will have you journaling the concerns, struggles, hopes, and fears you have in order to help you find the strength and knowledge to finally say "Bye Felicia" to the negative clutter in your home and the emotional clutter in your mind. Other steps will guide you through a series of fun and easy decluttering challenges, so you won't have to worry about what to keep or what you should let go of. And finally, by practicing the life-changing mindfulness exercises within your journal, you'll overcome the anxiety and fear that can come with letting go of those unused possessions and find the self-awareness necessary to stop the clutter from ever coming back.

In the end, this journey is about more than just getting rid of your clutter. It's about rediscovering yourself and gaining the insight and the tools necessary for living a happier, healthier, and more mindful life.

Now, it's time to get real and declutter all the emotional and physical crap that is getting in the way of the home and life of your dreams!

Definition of clutter in the dictionary:

(A lot of objects in) a state of being untidy.

My definition of clutter:

Any item that you do not use or love.

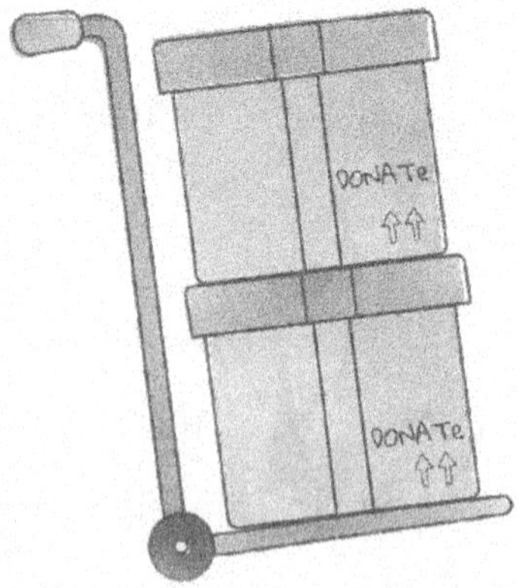
DONATe
DONATe

NAMAST'AY

HOME THIS WEEKEND AND
DECLUTTER SOME JUNK

STEP 1

Mindfulness

Zen level: Baby Yoda

mind·ful·ness

/ˈmīn(d)f(ə)lnəs/

noun

1. the quality or state of being conscious or aware of something. "Their mindfulness of the wider cinematic tradition."
2. a mental state achieved by focusing one's awareness in the present moment, while calmly acknowledging and accepting one's feelings, thoughts, and bodily sensations, used as a therapeutic technique.

Let's be real, I'm no Zen master, I don't meditate, huff essential oils, or practice yoga. I am, however, a strong believer in the power of *mindfulness*. Being mindful is simply taking time to be aware of your thoughts and feelings so you can recognize the effect they have on you, and if necessary, change them.

Example: If every time you need to clean the kitchen you get upset and think: *This isn't fair, I don't want to have to do housework after working all day*—you've made it into a horrible chore before you've even begun and now you're way less likely to actually clean the kitchen. If you catch yourself having these thoughts, acknowledge them, and then you can change them to: *If I spend fifteen minutes tidying the kitchen now, I'll* *have the rest of the night to relax.* **It's a small change in the way you self-talk, but it can have a huge impact on your motivation.**

Mindfulness helps me overcome irrational fears or negative thoughts in all kinds of situations, like when I am purging stuff I know I don't need, but am feeling stressed about getting rid of. Asking myself *Why am I feeling anxious right now?* and then finding the answer to that question is liberating. As a result of meditation, I can stay calm and rational in stressful situations and find the motivation to tackle difficult tasks.

That is why mindfulness is the first step in the decluttering process. The following pages are guided exercises to get to know yourself better. Take your time. As you move onto later steps, don't be afraid to come back to the beginning anytime you feel overwhelmed or anxious on your decluttering journey.

Look Where You Are Going, Not Where You Have Been

Happy memories are awesome, but we don't need actual physical items to keep our memories alive. Filling our home with yesterday's stuff means there is no room left for today and tomorrow.

Make a list of what you want to have in your future. Not physical things, but new memories you want to create or goals you want to achieve.

Write your Future

In the future I want to...

Every day, I want to feel...

Attitude and Gratitude

Be grateful for the things in your home that are useful, beautiful, or filled with happiness. This will make it easier to let go of the items that are not.

List all the items in your home that you love and appreciate. (With three children, I'm super grateful for my washing machine!)

I am grateful for...

The things that make me the happiest are...

If you feel discouraged during the decluttering process, come back to this page and remind yourself of the items that *really* matter.

Pass the Positivity Please

Nothing helps us focus on the end goal more than a little positive reinforcement.

Here are six awesome things about decluttering my home:

1.

2.

3.

4.

5.

6.

This Heart Needs Some Art

Doodle a self-portrait of a happy, organized you!

Just breathe.

Whenever you feel anxious during this process, close your eyes and practice this four-step breathing exercise. Also...you need to totally draw a picture in the middle of something that makes you feel calm and super Zen...

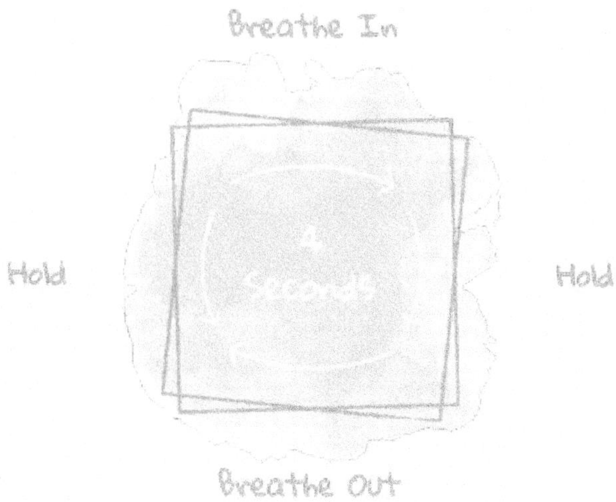

Did you close your eyes and practice breathing? Did you really? I don't believe you. Close them again and describe what you see...yes, I know it's all black...but *keep looking*. Do you see colors or shapes inside the black? Note: this may seem super weird but closing your eyes and breathing deeply is super calming, so just do it already!

I think I actually saw something when my eyes were closed! I saw...

Self-awareness

is the

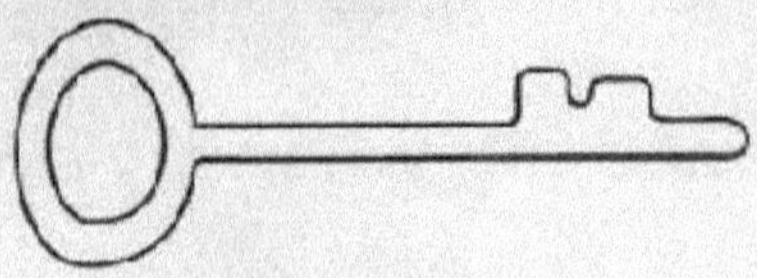

to self-mastery

- Gretchen Rubin -

STEP 2

Self-Awareness

In this step, you will explore how you think and feel about yourself. Are you kind to yourself or are you a giant bully? Do you clutter your mind with negative self-talk without even realizing it? Are you sabotaging your own success?

Now, what about your home? Are you being kind and loving to your home?

Perception shapes every aspect of our lives.

Do you remember the kitchen example in the last step? Notice the difference between: *This isn't fair, I don't want to have to do housework after working all day*, versus: *If I spend 15 minutes tidying the kitchen now, I'll have the rest of the night to relax.*

The kitchen is still messy, no matter which statement you use, but if you are thinking or feeling negatively, that's going to negatively impact how you respond to the situation. If two people were presented with the same kitchen mess, but one whined about it being unfair while the other looked forward to relaxing in fifteen minutes, which one do you think is more likely to both start and complete the task? Which one do you think is most likely going to wake up the next morning with the job unfinished, and an even messier kitchen the next night?

Awareness of the link between internal negativity and external clutter gives us an opportunity to change both.

But get ready, because this won't be just about how you perceive your messy kitchen or messy bedrooms. We are going to dig deep into how the thoughts and feelings you have about *yourself* impact the way your home looks.

So, let's get "shrinky"! The doctor is in. (Legal disclaimer: I am in no way a doctor of anything.)

It's All Too Much

Work, spouse, home, kids...sometimes life can be a *lot* to handle.

What is making me feel overwhelmed right now?

How will decluttering help me feel less overwhelmed?

Next to this trash can, make a list of things in your home you wish you could get rid of, but haven't been able to (it can totally include things that belong to your spouse or kids).

How Does Your Home Make You Feel Right Now?

When you look around at your home right now, how does it make you feel? Check off all that apply.

- Angry

- Stressed
- Depressed
- Anxious
- Frustrated
- Trapped
- Resentful
- Guilty
- Exhausted
- ______________________
- ______________________
- ______________________
- ______________________

How Do You Want Your Home to Make You Feel?

- Happy
- Organized
- Accomplished
- Calm
- Energized
- Proud
- Hopeful
- ______________________
- ______________________
- ______________________
- ______________________

Self-Perception Is Everything

This exercise can be tricky for someone new to mindfulness, so there is an example of a completed one on the next page.

We are trying to uncover the negative thoughts you harbor deep down about yourself and see how they could affect your actions.

The biggest issue with my home's current state is...

The worst thing about this is...

The worst thing about this is...

The worst thing about this is...

The worst thing about this is...

Core Negative Belief ↑

Let's Look at an Example of How Someone Might Have Filled in Those Blanks...

The biggest issue with my home's current state is...

My home is messy.

The worst thing about this is...

I don't have enough space for the things I want.

The worst thing about this is...

I'm not giving my children the home they deserve.

The worst thing about this is...

I am a bad mother.

The worst thing about this is...

I can't do anything right.

Core Negative Belief ↑

Sometimes our core negative beliefs about ourselves can even shape our lives in ways that we don't realize. Could that core belief that you "can't do anything right" actually be responsible for your messy home because it's causing you to give up or not even try? Absolutely. This is how we self-sabotage. Identifying that core negative belief is the first step to overcoming it.

Don’t you dare put the book down now! Don’t take a break on a negative thought like this.

Go to the next page RIGHT NOW!

It’s time to be kind to yourself and practice some positive self-talk.

Practice kindness to yourself

Be Your Own Best Friend, Not Your Own Worst Enemy

The core negative belief I discovered about myself is...

What if that belief *isn't true at all* and is only your negative perception of yourself?

It's time to tell that nasty inner voice to shut it! List five ways that you are totally awesome!

My core negative belief isn't true because...

1. ______________________________
2. ______________________________
3. ______________________________
4. ______________________________
5. ______________________________

Stop the Name Calling

Put your inner bully in time out and circle some kind words about yourself.

responsible
FRIENDLY
genuine
FUNNY
DARING
brave
loving
INSPIRING
smart
silly
wise
talented
HARDWORKING
intuitive
kind
HUMBLE

Are You Willing to Wait?

You have the power to drastically improve your life and your mood even *before* you declutter or organize at all.

It starts with changing your thoughts.

Write the goal you have for your home in the top corner of this diamond.

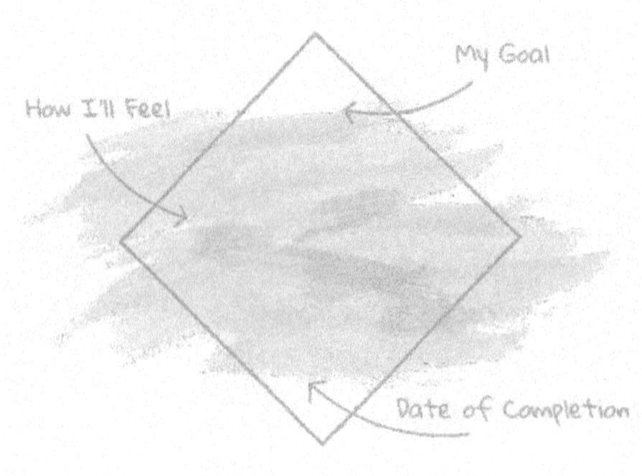

Now, using just one word, write in the middle how achieving this goal will make you feel about yourself.

In the bottom corner, write the date you want to achieve your goal by.

Now, get ready for this...*scratch out your goal!*

Why would you wait until that date to feel that way about yourself?

Choose to feel that way about yourself *right now*, regardless of your goal.

positive self-image
and positive self-talk
are key to making big
dreams come true

Anonymous

It's Time to Say Bye-Bye to the House Hate

What have you grown to hate about your home? Not enough storage? Never-ending surface clutter? Need an extra bedroom? Let it all out in this space...it's super cathartic.

Now...stop focusing on the negative!

Grab a bright and bold pen, and **scratch those negative things out**.

Write down the things you LOVE about your home in the space below. Maybe it has great bones, or lots of natural light. Write at least one positive for each negative thing you wrote down.

You and your home may not be perfect, but it's time to stop obsessing about what is wrong, and instead **bloom where you are planted**.

Just writing down your goals means you're halfway to accomplishing them

Clutterbug

STEP 3

Set Goals

The simple act of writing down a goal and then breaking that goal into smaller steps is the secret behind the success of so many high achievers.

It may seem unnecessary to write your goals down on paper because you already have them in your head, but I promise you, writing it down changes it from an idea that is just hanging out in the back of your mind into a real life goal. Taking the time to write down what you want in life transforms vague wishes into a concrete goals that are meant to be achieved.

In this step, we will explore what you *really* want from your home and how achieving these goals will improve your day-to-day life. Your goal may be to live in a clean and clutter-free home, but what are you really looking to gain in achieving that goal?

Understanding your goals on a deeper level can help to reveal the underlying motivations influencing you in the first place. Perhaps you are looking for more time. Maybe it's about wanting less stress or a more beautiful home. Whatever the reasons, let your feelings flow. Get ready to dig deep into what your biggest goals and dreams are really saying about your motivation and overall lifestyle.

The goal for my home is...

(write your goal in the banner below)

Success Starts with an End Goal

What is my decluttering goal? Why do I want a clutter-free home?

____

____

____

____

____

____

____

____

How will achieving this goal make me feel about myself?

____

____

Spoiler alert...this is *really* your end goal.)

↑

"Break It Down...Oh Oh Oh Oh..." in the Wise Words of MC Hammer

You wrote down your big important goal, now let's...*break it down.*

List at least TEN steps that you will need to complete to achieve it. Example: if you want to declutter your entire home, your steps may include "get thirty large boxes" or "rent a U-Haul truck to transport donations."

My ten steps are:

1

2

3

4

5

6

7

8

9

10

Get Your Priorities Straight

Truth time: Your to-do list is probably super unrealistic.

Don't overestimate how much you can accomplish in a short amount of time. Let's prioritize your list so you don't get discouraged.

The five steps from the last page that will have the biggest impact on me and my home are:

1.

2.

3.

4.

5.

What are some FUN goals you have for yourself? Fill these paper scraps with places you want to travel or new hobbies you want to try.

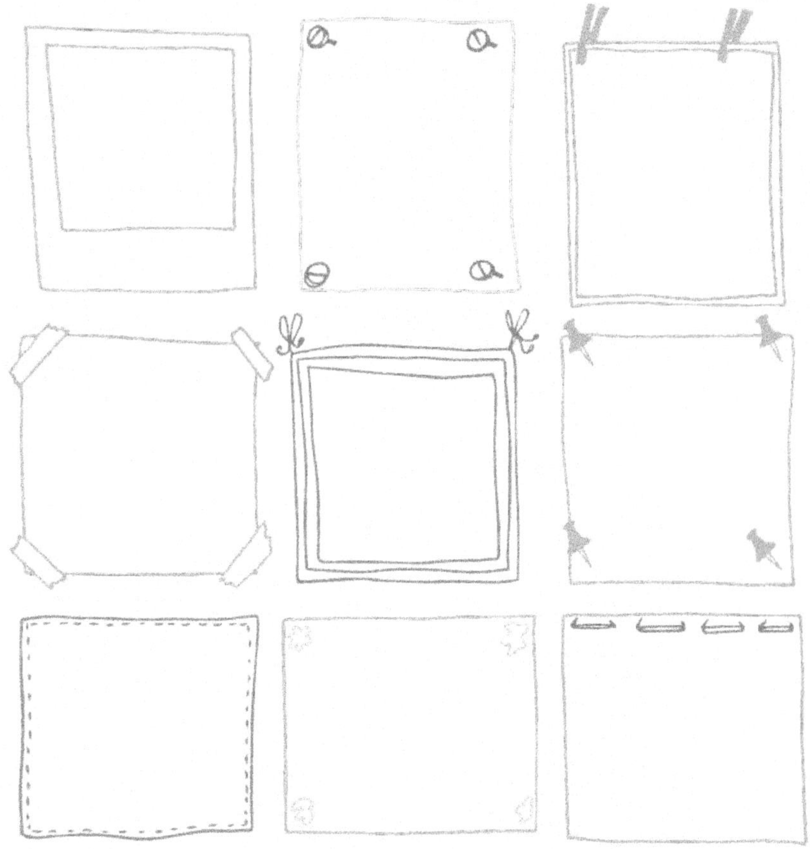

DREAM BIG
AND
DARE TO
FAIL

STEP 4

Dream Big

Dreams and goals go hand in hand. I want you to be able to dream big, but also have the ability to break your big dreams and goals down into manageable and attainable chunks.

Step 3 was about identifying the goal or goals that fix your immediate household needs and understanding the importance of breaking down a big goal into smaller, short term goals.

Step 4 is about giving yourself the freedom to dream big...*really* big. What is your long term dream for your current home?

Go room by room. Explore how you want your home to look and function for years to come.

Do you want the kitchen to energize you or feel relaxing and cozy? Do you want your living room to feel like an adult oasis or a fun family gathering spot?

Writing down your dream for each space will make it 75 percent more likely to come true (I heard this somewhere from someone, so let's just go with it).

Room by Room Dream Guide

Room 1: Bedroom

My dream bedroom looks like:

My dream bedroom makes me feel:

My dream bedroom is filled with:

My dream bedroom is used for:

Room 2: Bathroom

My dream bathroom looks like:

My dream bathroom makes me feel:

My dream bathroom is filled with:

My dream bathroom is used for:

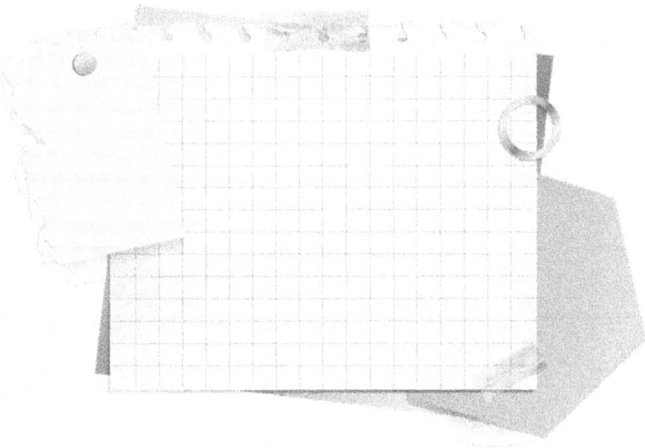

Room 3: Living Room

My dream living room looks like:

My dream living room makes me feel:

My dream living room is filled with:

My dream living room is used for:

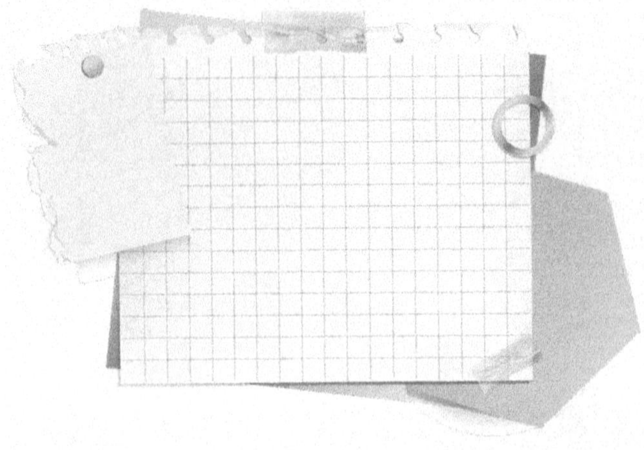

Room 4: Kitchen

My dream kitchen looks like:

My dream kitchen makes me feel:

My dream kitchen is filled with:

My dream kitchen is used for:

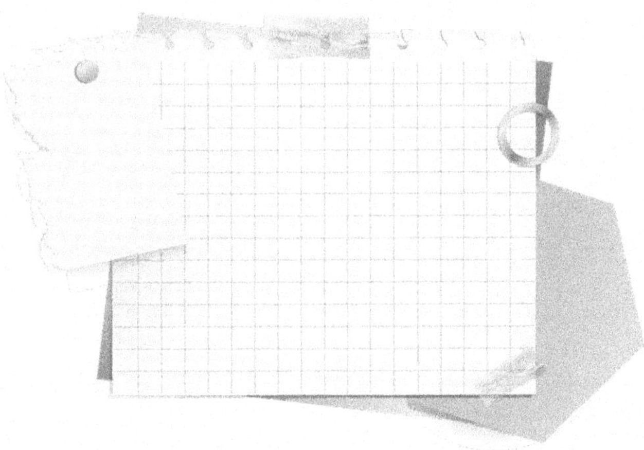

Room 5: ______

My dream ______ looks:

My dream ______ makes me feel:

My dream ______ is filled with:

My dream _______ is used for:

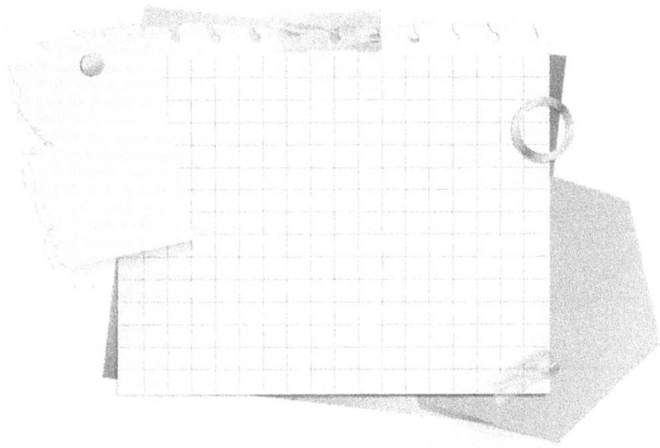

Room 6: _______

My dream _______ looks:

My dream _______ makes me feel:

My dream ______ is filled with:

My dream ______ is used for:

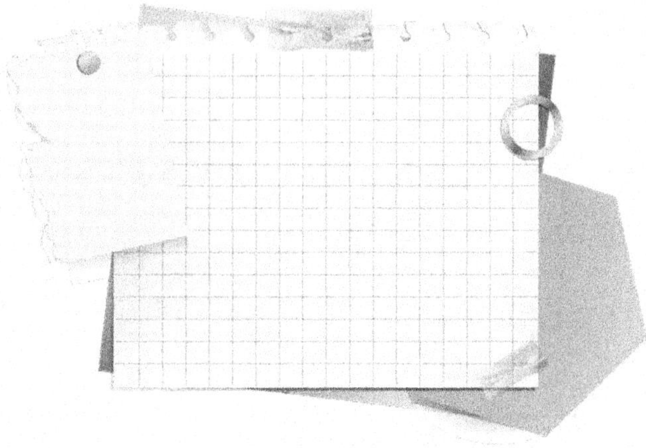

Play Favorites

Which room do you want to do first? Draw a picture of how you want that space to look on the next page.

The space I want to do first is...

I want this space to look like...

Draw a picture of your space.

We have nothing to fear except fear itself
Franklin Roosevelt

STEP 5

The Meaning Behind the Mess

There Is Always a Meaning Behind the Mess

I challenge you to look deep inside yourself and discover that hidden meaning behind your clutter.

Do you (now or in the past) struggle financially, and so letting go of "stuff" feels like wasting money? Have you suffered a loss or trauma and now all your possessions provide a feeling of safety and security? Do you hold onto "useful" items you feel make your life easier, even though it adds to the clutter making your life worse? Did you once lose something important to you, and now struggle to put things away for fear you may lose or forget about them?

Here's a thought that could either be a revelation or, really hard to accept. **Often, our attachment to our belongings comes from an underlying insecurity or fear.** Fear of loss, fear of failure, fear of the unknown, or fear of making a mistake.

Perhaps you are someone who subconsciously uses their possessions to define themselves or reinforce upon others an image you want to convey. For example, maybe you are someone who hangs onto or collects children's items to reinforce that you are a good parent. Maybe you have an abundance of books to reinforce you are intelligent, artsy, or educated?

Simply by understanding yourself better and the "why" behind your struggle with clutter, you can fight back and overcome the fear and anxiety that has held you back from the home and life you deserve.

Take a deep breath. Sharpen your pencil. Get ready to get *real* with yourself.

Finding Your "Why"

Think about something in your home that it would be hard to get rid of, even though you don't necessarily like or use it.

Why are you reluctant to let go?

Examples: Does it feel wasteful to get rid of something that isn't garbage? Do you worry you will need to spend money to replace it some day? Do you feel guilty because it was a gift?

An item that would be hard for me to let go of is...

It's hard for me to let go because...

Getting rid of it makes me feel anxious because...

Getting rid of it makes me feel guilty because...

Don't Be Such a Scaredy Cat

Decluttering can be stressful, but that stress comes from fear and not from the physical act of decluttering. Fear of failure, fear of regret, fear of making a mistake. **Facing your fear is so much harder to overcome than the work of decluttering.**

Think of an item in your home that would cause you real anxiety to donate.

Now, imagine you just did. Eek!

The WORST thing that would actually happen if I let this item go is...

____

____

____

____

____

____

Is the worst thing really that bad? Is it worse than having a messy, cluttered home? How can you get past this fear?

____

____

____

____

____

____

You Are NOT What You Own

Humans are weird. We buy and hold onto items that reinforce beliefs about ourselves, or to try and demonstrate those beliefs to others. Example: "I love owning a lot of books because they make me feel intelligent and well-read" or "I enjoy buying my children new toys because I like feeling like a good parent" or "I like having a lot of reusable water bottles because it feels good to be environmentally concious."

I think my desire to have a lot of says that I am...

____

____

____

____

____

____

____

I don't really need the physical items to feel that way about myself because...

____

____

____

____

____

____

____

Childhood Connection

How could your childhood impact how your home looks now?

Did your parents struggle with clutter? Were you taught how to clean and organize? Were you called "messy" or "lazy" as a child?

My childhood affects my current home because...

Check all that apply:

- As an adult, I am in control of my own life
- I am not my parents
- I am no longer a child
- I have the ability to change
- I am not messy
- I am super awesome

Hint: You are supposed to check all of the circles!

The space in which we live should be for the person we are becoming now, not the person that we were in the past

-Marie Kondo-

STEP 6

Feel the Urge to Purge

Decluttering is really fun (no, for reals, it really is). Once you have pinpointed the underlying reason that made letting go feel uncomfortable or difficult in the past, you can embrace the feel-good emotions that come with moving forward.

DECLUTTERING IS ALL ABOUT LETTING GO OF THE PAST TO MAKE ROOM FOR THE PRESENT AND THE FUTURE.

Decluttering is the process of simplifying your life and making space for the things that really matter to you. When we have too much stuff, our actual special or prized possessions are smothered and made invisible. Just like the old saying "you can't see the forest for the trees," you truly can't see and appreciate your beautiful and beloved items when there are just too many things crowding the space. Less really is more.

Because you look at your home every day, all the "stuff" in it has probably become invisible to you. Just like you often need a "fresh pair of eyes" to find your spelling mistakes, you often can't see your own clutter either!

Step 6 will force you to take off the blinders and inventory of the invisible clutter in your home. There's also some fun "warm up" decluttering exercises to show you how rewarding it really is!

Invisible Clutter

Grab your phone and snap a photo of any space you want. Looking at the picture rather than looking at the room or closet in person will allow you to see it from an outsider's perspective. It's like when I see a photo of myself on Facebook and I'm like "WTH...Why do I have five chins and look like the Stay Puft Marshmallow Man?" A photo can be denial-crushing. What clutter do you see that you might not have noticed before?

Looking at a picture of my space, I notice....

____

____

____

____

____

____

____

My space will look less chaotic if I remove...

____

____

____

____

____

____

____

I'm a Hidey Hoarder

Clutter isn't just stuff laying around, it's hidden everywhere in your house.

Get snoopy and peak inside drawers and cabinets to spot items that you haven't used in the last year.

When I looked inside my hidden spaces, I was shocked to find...

The drawer in my home that is the messiest is filled with...

The closet in my home that is the messiest is filled with...

you don't
need more space
you need
less stuff

Garbage Bag Therapy

Warm up your urge to purge!

Grab two bags, one for garbage and one for recycling. Set a timer for five minutes... On your mark, get set, GO!

Search your home for actual garbage: Expired medication, broken items, old papers, receipts, expired food, and empty food wrappers.

I filled my bag with...

OMG, that was actual garbage just sitting around your house!

Now go put it where it belongs.

21-Item Toss

Let's toss some stuff! This exercise is super fun, I promise.

Go find 21 items you can toss or donate. Does 21 sound like a lot? It's easier than you think!

Look for clothing you don't wear, old greeting cards, kids' artwork, or Christmas mugs you never even use—even at Christmas! Do you have lotions that were gifted to you years ago still sitting in the back of the bathroom closet? It's time to say goodbye. I know you can find 21 things fast!

On your mark, get set....GO!

Look what I tossed:

1. ______________________________
2. ______________________________
3. ______________________________
4. ______________________________
5. ______________________________
6. ______________________________
7. ______________________________
8. ______________________________
9. ______________________________
10. ______________________________
11. ______________________________

12. ____

13. ____

14. ____

15. ____

16. ____

17. ____

18. ____

19. ____

20. ____

21. ____

Look at all
my stuff
that used to
be money

1.

STEP 7

The Cost of Clutter

Have you ever taken the time to really think about what your clutter is costing you?

I don't mean the money you spent to buy these items (although that IS a depressing thought). I mean the *emotional amount* it is taxing you.

How does it tax you? Ask yourself:

Do I fight with my spouse or partner over the mess?

Do I find myself resenting my home or family because of the clutter?

Do I have less free time because I am always cleaning and tidying (or avoiding cleaning and tidying)?

Do I make excuses to leave the house just to avoid looking at the mess or do I escape it by watching television or surfing the web?

Do I miss out on relationships with friends and family because I am too embarrassed to have people over?

These are not small concerns. Clutter clearly comes with significant costs to your happiness and lifestyle. What is that worth to you?

When you see it for more than just the dollar amount you paid for it, it will be much easier to justify letting these possessions go.

In this step, *really* think about the ways in which your extra stuff takes from you.

It's Costing More to Keep Than I Paid for It

How my clutter is costing me:

Letting go of unused items will give me...

Less Stuff Equals More Love

Frustration, anger, and resentment grow easily out of arguments around clutter and chores. It is a huge drain on too many relationships. By eliminating (or even just reducing) the clutter, you can stop pointing fingers and playing the blame game. It's time to shift the focus on a happier and healthier relationship.

Sometimes I feel angry or resentful toward my spouse because...

____

____

____

Letting go of my unused items will improve my relationship with my spouse because...

____

____

____

____

A clean and clutter-free home will improve my other relationships because...

____

____

____

____

____

____

Mood Over Matter

You don't need to be in a relationship for clutter to exploit negative and toxic emotions. We are all our own worst enemies. Cluttered and chaotic environments will create **stress, anxiety, and depression** in anyone's mind.

When I look around at the messy areas of my home, I feel...

____

____

____

____

____

____

____

____

____

How will having a clutter-free home affect my mood?

____

____

____

____

____

____

What can I do to boost my happiness right now? (Circle something and do it right now!)

Eat A Snack

Go For A Walk

Call A Friend

Have A Nap

Have A Bath

Make A Hot Drink

Hug Someone

Paint My Nails

Listen To Music

Light A Candle

When we really delve into
the reasons why we can't
let something go,
there are only two:
attachment to the past
or fear of the future.
-Marie Kondo

STEP 8

Overcoming Obstacles

We all make excuses for why we hold onto things in our home that we know we really don't need. These excuses are obstacles in the way of having that clean and organized home you deserve. But what if trying to overcome the excuse causes great fear and anxiety?

In working with my many clients I have found that, in most cases, excuses are usually about something completely unrelated to what the client believes the problem to be. When confronted with cleaning or purging, sometimes unresolved issues totally unrelated to housework can cause cleaning to become overwhelming and debilitating.

What, if any, could be your unresolved issues hiding behind the excuses?

In this step, we are going to break down some of the common purging obstacles, so you can work through and overcome these challenges easily.

As you declutter, there will be times that you struggle, and that is ok! Remember to go back and reread "Step 5: The Meaning Behind Your Mess" before coming back to this step and working through the obstacle.

Practice Makes Perfect

When you come across something that is difficult to let go, navigate those uncomfortable feelings by asking these questions:

Why haven't I let go of my unused clutter before?

Why do I procrastinate tidying and decluttering?

What is the worst that could happen if I donated something that I needed later?

How is my clutter preventing me from living my best life?

How can I overcome my excuses and make the changes I know I need?

Eventually you will navigate around the uncomfortable feelings without thinking about them!

NOT ALL CLUTTER IS THE SAME.

LET'S LOOK AT THE COMMON FORMS OF CLUTTER AND THE UNIQUE MENTAL OBSTACLES THAT PREVENT YOU FROM GETTING RID OF THEM.

Guilty Clutter
A collection of unwanted items you only keep out of obligation.

This could be items passed down from loved ones or gifts you have received. What clutter do you not want or need, but feel guilty about purging?

The first guilty clutter item that comes to mind is...

____

____

____

____

I got this item from...

____

____

____

____

I feel like I need to keep it because...

____

____

____

____

I'm not honoring this item in the way it deserves because...

I could honor this item better by giving it to someone I know who would love or use it, or by donating it to charity. Some places or people who I could give this to are...

Sentimental Clutter
Items that have a deep meaning or value to you but aren't necessarily useful and take up valuable space.

This could include children's artwork or mementoes from your own childhood.

A piece of sentimental clutter I own is...

It is sentimental to me because...

____

____

____

____

____

____

____

Letting go of the item won't let go of the memory because...

What was holding me back from releasing sentimental clutter in the past?

Why should I let go of more sentimental items?

Tip: Take a picture of sentimental items before letting them go.

Useful Clutter
A collection of "good" things that are rarely or never used.

If I had a dollar for every time a client said to me "but I may need this someday," I'd be hella rich. You may think your home is not filled with actual clutter because you only have things that are good and useful. However, a collection of useful things (I'm looking at you kitchen and workshop) that are never or rarely used is still just *clutter*.

I define clutter as "items that are not being used and/or an excess of items that do not have a proper home."

Remember, filling your home with too many "useful" but unused things can make your living space useless.

Some items I have that may be "useful" but I never use are...

Even though I never use these items, I'm reluctant to let go because...

These items are not worth the space they take and the stress they cause because...

Expensive Clutter
Things you won't purge because you spent a lot of money on them.

It sucks to feel like you are wasting money, but the truth is, our stuff isn't worth today what we paid for it in the past. Does anxiety about wasting money stop you from decluttering your home?

Keeping an item around does not make you richer. Letting it go doesn't cost you anything.

Items that I am keeping just because they were expensive are...

These items are not making me richer because...

I should let these items go because...

I could sell, donate, or give these items to a friend. I think I should...

Perfectionism Paralysis

During the decluttering process, the fear of making a mistake can be a huge obstacle. This fear most often occurs in people who are perfectionists or in someone who fears losing control.

I may be a perfectionist because...

Why do I put so much pressure on myself?

What household tasks have I been putting off until I can "do them perfectly"?

How can I let go of some control and embrace "good enough" when it comes to my home?

*Love the life you have
while you create the life
of your dreams*

\- Hal Elrod

It's not about "finding" the time

It's about making the time

STEP 9

Making Time for What Matters

So far, you have journaled about the challenges which have previously contributed to your clutter. You have also journaled about the goals and dreams you have for your home. Now it's time to focus on making the time to turn those goals into reality.

I know that you think you are already too busy. I feel you; I am busy too. We are all busy, but, just like we have to make time for our kids, friends, and spouses, we need to make time for our homes. It's important to always make time for what really matters. Doesn't your home matter?

This step is a double whammy. It is all about becoming more aware of how you spend your time and how you can better use that time to accomplish your goals and dreams. Any goal can be accomplished in as little as fifteen minutes a day. You're going to find that it is surprisingly easy to make space in both your home and in your schedule, so let's go make an extra fifteen minutes a day.

Identify Your Time Suckers

If you want to have more free time, you gotta weed out the time suckers in your life. Do you spend hours scrolling through Facebook posts from people you don't even like? Are you getting distracted by terrible afternoon television that you don't even enjoy watching? Does a five-minute game of Candy Crush easily become two hours without you even realizing it?

Be aware of how you spend your time. Write down those time wasters in your life.

I waste precious time by...

____

____

____

____

____

How can you limit these time wasters? Try setting a timer before you go on social media or challenging yourself to give up an online video game altogether.

I can limit my time wasters by...

____

____

____

____

____

It's a Date!

In Step 3, you set a goal and *broke it down* into smaller, manageable tasks. Grab your calendar and pick a time in the next seven days to complete just one of those smaller tasks.

No more excuses, no more procrastinating.

Today's Date: ______

What will I accomplish?

____

____

____

____

____

____

____

____

____

I am going to start on this date...

I will be done by...

The supplies I need are...

If your tasks will take longer than fifteen minutes to complete, try breaking them down even further. Repeat this exercise again next week until your list is done. If you start to feel more ambitious, do two a week, or...try the next exercise.

Short Term Pain for Long Term Gain

It's time to tackle a bigger project! Making the time for this does mean a bit more time and effort in the short term, but the long term payoff is more than worth it!

Look back to Step 5: Dream Big.

The space I wanted to declutter first is: ______.

I am going to start decluttering this space on this date: ______.

Break down this dream into small, fifteen-minute decluttering tasks. Be realistic. Trying to do it all at once can be exhausting and discouraging, so try just doing one or two small tasks a day.

My decluttering schedule for this space is:

Day/Time		Task	
Day/Time		Task	
Day/Time		Task	
Day/Time		Task	
Day/Time		Task	

do something today that your future self will thank you for

STEP 10

Creating Motivation

Before we jump into even bigger decluttering challenges, we need to have a talk about motivation.

Let's face it, motivation is critical to the decluttering process because achieving the home of your dreams is going to take time and effort. You will definitely have days or even *weeks* when you won't feel like decluttering anymore. Proper motivation will keep you moving forward when the going gets tough. I'm going to show you some easy ways to get started, even on those days you feel like staying in bed and crushing some Netflix. The amazing thing about motivation is, once you get started, it's the results and rewards that will keep you going.

I know what I am talking about. As a master procrastinator, I need all the motivation I can get. The motivation techniques I will guide you through here in Step 10 are the very ones I use in my own life. It's how I get my difficult to-do lists done, even when a new season of my favorite show just gets released!

Just for funsies, draw a mountain with stick figure you at the top!

NAG Yourself

This first, super-easy motivation technique will help you push through the procrastination to actually get your to-do list done. I call it the NAG yourself technique!

N is for NOTE. Each and every day, write yourself a note with five easy and realistic tasks you want to accomplish that day. Leave it somewhere visual. Example: Make the bed, wash the dishes, do one load of laundry, declutter one bathroom drawer, declutter expired medicine.

Today I am going to:

1.
2.
3.
4.
5.
6.

The best place to put my daily to-do list is...

____

____

____

____

____

A is for ALARM. Set alarms to go off throughout the day to remind you to tackle something on your list. Will that be annoying? Yes it will! Will it be effective? Yes it will!

Write down each of your five tasks again and write the time beside it that the alarm should go off to remind you.

The best time to complete each of my tasks is...

Time	Task
Time	Task
Time	Task
Time	Task
Time	Task

G is for GIFT. Reward yourself when you get each of your five items accomplished! This gift shouldn't have a monetary value (no you can't use this as an excuse to shop every day and bring *more* objects into your home); rather, it's about doing something kind for yourself as a reward.

I can reward myself by...

Examples: Have a bubble bath, enjoy a sweet treat, take a walk, watch a movie etc.

Accountability

Having an accountability partner is an amazing way to stay motivated. Find someone, or even a group of people, with whom you can share your goals, and then connect with them daily, weekly, or monthly. Your accountability partner can be a friend, family member or even a Facebook group!

My accountability partner could be...

Having accountability will help me because...

I can help someone else be accountable by...

One Minute Rule

If something takes one minute or less, do it now. We all procrastinate but ignoring or putting off one-minute tasks can quickly add up to hours of work.

Wiping down the kitchen counter, putting dirty clothes in the hamper, putting your dirty dishes in the dishwasher, hanging up your coat and putting your shoes away when you come home, and throwing out empty food containers are all activities that take a minute or less.

Tasks I can accomplish in sixty seconds or less include...

1.

2.

3.

4.

5.

Habit Stacking

Habit stacking combines new, desired habits with an existing daily habit.

Examples:

- When you make a pot of coffee, write a to-do list while it brews.
- When you brush your teeth, tidy the bathroom or wipe down the counter.
- While you're waiting for dinner to cook, tidy the kitchen or declutter a drawer.

Some new habits I want to start are...

I can pair a new habit with an old one by...

Old Habit	New Habit

SMALL STEPS EVERY DAY

It's hard to procrastinate

when someone is counting on you

It's easy to let yourself down, but really

difficult to let down others.

STEP 11

How to Declutter the Right Way

You mean there's a right and a wrong way? *How do I do it right?* I'm glad you asked.

Part 1: Pick a *small* area of your home, such as a drawer or closet. If you are dealing with a very cluttered room, choose just one corner or area at a time. Take everything out and put in a pile.

Part 2: Get three bags or boxes, one labelled "keep," one labelled "donate," and one for "trash/recycling."

Part 3: Start sorting into the keep, donate, or trash piles. Resist the urge to sort into lots of smaller categories—the first step is just to get rid of the clutter.

Do not overcomplicate this process or you could become overwhelmed. As you sort, ask yourself is "Have I used this in the past twelve months?" If the answer is no, it's gotta go.

Something that is useful is not always necessary. If you haven't used it in the past twelve months, that item is actually *taking* value from your life by stealing your time, space, and mental storage. This step is all about letting go of the unimportant items you've been hoarding so that your important and special things are honored and easy to find.

Part 4: Find homes for the items you intend to keep, and donate or trash/recycle the rest *immediately*.

I Forgot I Even Owned That

Take a look inside your cabinets and closets to find one larger item that you haven't used in more than twelve months. Example: a small kitchen appliance, pair of boots, serving platter, broken vacuum, etc.

I haven't used ____________ in over a year, but I haven't gotten rid of it because...

When I donate this item, I'll have more space for...

What's the BIGGEST item in your home that you really never use? In my home, it's the treadmill. Fantasy Cas is going to start running. Real life Cas can barely walk to the end of the driveway.

The biggest item that never gets used is...

Do you have something that "Fantasy You" was going to use, but in reality, you probably never will? Examples: Scrapbooking supplies, exercise equipment, a bread maker, etc.

Fantasy me is in denial about...

The sole purpose of the bedroom is to melt away any stressors.

Jonathan Scott

STEP 12

Declutter Your Bedroom

The master bedroom is always the first space I recommend decluttering because I truly believe it will have the biggest impact on your life.

Your bedroom is the last thing you see each night before you fall asleep and the first thing you see when you open your eyes in the morning. A messy, cluttered, and chaotic bedroom can make it difficult to relax and fall asleep, or zap your energy, motivation and happiness when you wake up. Cluttered and messy rooms can also affect your health because you're breathing in dust and other allergens as you sleep.

Raise your hand if you want a healthy, tidy bedroom!

Your bedroom should help you fall asleep faster at night and allow you to wake up rested and ready to take on the day.

In this step, I challenge you to make your bedroom a priority. Push yourself to let go of even more items than the challenges include.

This is your chance to have the bedroom oasis you deserve. You got this!

Goodbye Chaos, Hello Clean

What is and isn't working in my bedroom?

Grab a bag or a box and pack up the following for charity or the garbage:

- 15 tops (shirts, sweaters, tanks) that don't look great on you or no longer fit
- 5 bottoms (pants, shorts, or skirts) that you never wear or no longer fit
- 2 old pairs of pajamas that look too worn
- 5 pairs of underwear that have seen better days
- 2 bras that poke you or just don't fit right anymore
- 10 holey or single socks missing their pairs
- 5 accessories that are collecting dust, i.e., ties, belts, hats, scarves, jewelry

Fill the newfound space from this purge with stuff you couldn't put away before!

I found this decluttering challenge _______________ because...

____

____

____

____

____

____

____

____

____

____

____

Bye, Bye Bedroom Blues

Before I decluttered, my bedroom made me feel...

Decluttering my bedroom makes me feel...

____

In order to maintain a tidy bedroom, I need to...

- Make my bed every day
- Do ____ loads of laundry each week
- Take 5 minutes each night to clear off surfaces
- Put away laundry / dirty laundry in the hamper
- ____________________
- ____________________
- ____________________
- ____________________

Kitchens
are made for
bringing families
together

STEP 13

Declutter Your Kitchen

The kitchen is the one space in every home that gets messy faster than any other room. Obviously, we cook and eat in our kitchens, but it's also a landing spot for the entire family and their stuff. The kitchen is the heart of a home and when that heart is cluttered and disorganized, it flows out of the kitchen and spreads throughout the entire home.

Decluttering the kitchen will do so much more than just make it *look* better.

Having less mess in your kitchen means that preparing meals will be easier, cleaning up will be faster, and there will be more space for enjoying family time together. Cooking, eating, or socializing in a clean and tidy kitchen is always so much more enjoyable.

Completing these challenges will make decluttering your kitchen as pain-free as possible. Remember to focus on your end goal as you work. Envision how you want your kitchen to feel and function and ask yourself, "Is this item helping or hindering that vision?" As explored in earlier steps, you can be reluctant to let go of an underused cooking gadget or small appliance because you "might use it someday." If it isn't being used, it's just taking up valuable space, and making your kitchen less functional.

Clutter-Free Cooking Starts Here

What is and isn't currently working in my kitchen?

Grab a box and fill it with the following items to donate or trash/recycle:

- 5 food storage containers without lids or extra lids with no container

- 1 pot or pan you never use (like that scratched one with the wobbly handle)
- 1 small kitchen appliance that hasn't been used in that last twelve months
- 2 large utensils that you don't need (i.e., extra serving spoons, potato mashers, etc.)
- 3 mismatched or chipped mugs that are just collecting dust
- 1 large serving tray or bowl that hasn't been used in the last twelve months
- 5 extras such as unused aprons, placemats, dishcloths, or dishes
- Expired food in the fridge and pantry

I was also able to get rid of...

___

___

___

___

___

___

___

___

___

___

Clear Counter Challenge

If you aren't careful, any flat surface is an invitation to set random things down and clutter quickly attracts more clutter.

My kitchen counter can often get cluttered because...

____

____

____

____

____

How can I reduce the amount of clutter on my counter in the future?

____

____

____

____

____

I want to make a clean and tidy kitchen a priority because...

____

____

____

____

____

Decluttering isn't

a chore, it's a

gift to yourself.

– Clutterbug –

Soap is to the body

·what laughter is to the·

Soul.

STEP 14

Declutter Your Bathroom

Bathrooms are often so neglected when it comes to decluttering and organizing, probably because they are usually out of the way and out of sight compared to the rest of the home. When you think about it, however, they get more traffic than any other area of your home.

To me, bathrooms are a place of health and wellness. Besides the *obvious* reasons—we use bathrooms everyday—they are also the place where we get clean and fresh to face the day, and get ready for bed each night. It's where we wash away dirt and troubles and pamper and treat ourselves with lotions, masks, and relaxing bubble baths. Bathrooms transform our appearance and mindset into the best versions of ourselves (isn't that so much nicer than just thinking of our bathrooms as the place to take a poop?).

With the abundance of products we use to make ourselves clean and pretty, bathrooms can get messy fast, so it's important to keep them organized.

I want your bathroom to feel like a luxury spa. I want you to easily find your favorite products and be able to put them away when you're done without a second thought. An organized bathroom will save you time and effort each and every day, so it's a wonderful investment of your time.

When decluttering your bathroom, be ruthless. Like in your kitchen, if you don't use certain products, let them go, even if they were pricey.

Having less will mean the products that you actually use, and love, are more visible and easy to access and you no longer have to struggle with limited space.

It's time to focus on pampering yourself and make self-care a priority.

It Rubs the Lotion on Its Skin

It's time to let go of those unused lotions, potions, and almost-empty bottles of goo in your bathroom! Grab a trash bag and say goodbye to:

- 5 makeup items that just don't look good on you
- 4 lotions that you never use (if unopened, donate to a women's shelter)
- 3 expired medication or first aid products
- 2 old, stained or ripped bath towels
- 1 hair styling tool you never use (yes, I'm talking about those hot rollers)
- Old toothbrushes and empty toothpaste tubes
- Empty shampoo bottles in the shower

When my bathroom counter is clutter-free, life will be easier because...

____

____

____

____

____

____

____

Be honest, how many empty containers of shampoo, conditioner, body wash, lotions and toothpaste did you find?

____

So Fresh and So Clean, Clean.

Now that I have decluttered my bathroom...

- I'm motivated to keep going
- It feels cleaner/sanitary
- I'm happy to have more space
- I realize how many unused items I had
- I am finally content to let guests' use it
- I take more time to relax in the shower/bath
- ______________________
- ______________________
- ______________________
- ______________________
- ______________________

Create a five-minute daily tidy up routine for your bathroom to keep it clean.

- Wipe down counter/sink
- Put products away
- ______________________
- ______________________
- ______________________
- ______________________
- ______________________
- ______________________

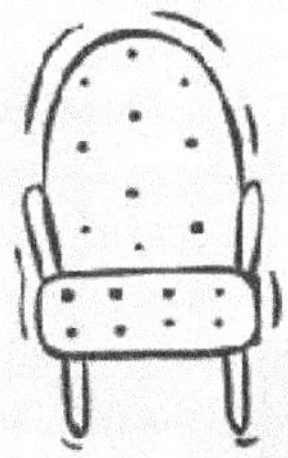

Living rooms are
for living, not
storing your stuff

STEP 15

Declutter Your Living Room

Your living room should invite you to "come in and relax," not scream "Hi, I'm abused by a million children and their pets; and don't mind the sofa, it's for laundry, not sitting."

Living rooms are multi-functional spaces. They are where you watch television, entertain guests, read books, have children play with toys, play board games or video games, and store family memories. With so much going on in one room, it's no wonder it can become pretty cluttered.

This is probably the space that you always tidy and clean before company comes over, but when is the last time you actually decluttered this space?

In this step we are going to make some much needed *living* room in your living room. Did you like that play on words there? I'm so punny.

Happy Little Living Room Thoughts

Let's take a second to focus on the great stuff about your space!

The things I love about my living room are...

I want my living room to be a place for...

I want my living room to feel...

- Relaxed

- Energized
- Happy
- Proud
- Organized
- Cozy
- Family Friendly
- ______________________
- ______________________
- ______________________
- ______________________
- ______________________
- ______________________
- ______________________
- ______________________
- ______________________
- ______________________
- ______________________
- ______________________

Rein in the Random

Living rooms accumulate a lot of random clutter. It's time to rein it in! Start by letting go of the following:

- 5 random unloved decor items such as knick knacks or picture frames
- 5 books, magazines, or old newspapers you'll never read again
- 3 board games you never play
- 3 unused tech items such as old remotes, outdated video games, DVDs or old cell phones
- 2 more random items that need to leave this room

What else do you keep in your living room?

My living room is also home to my...

___

___

___

___

___

___

___

___

___

___

___

___

The most random things in my living room are…

LESS STUFF
— EQUALS —
MORE LIFE

Let's Make This Personal

Doodle a design of your dream feature wall for this room. It could be a fireplace, family photo gallery, artwork, or anything else to make your living room personalized and pretty.

An avalanche of toys invites emotional disconnect and a sense of overwhelm

- Dr. Kim John Payne -

STEP 16

Declutter Kids' Toys

Children get overwhelmed with clutter too. The less toys your children see, the more they will actually play with what they have. Conversely, when there is an overabundance of toys to choose from, it smothers their creativity and motivation to play.

The act of purging toys is going to be hard for you, and it's probably even harder for your children. Remember though, you are doing your child a favor by thinning out the toys. Don't feel bad; you are teaching them valuable life lessons.

First, having less will make it easier for them to organize and tidy their toys all by themselves. Having less also instils respect and gratitude for what they do have. Lastly, the creative play unleashed by the presence of fewer distracting toys will stimulate your child's mind...or so the smarty pants scientists say.

"I'm Doing This for Your Own Good."

Grab a box and donate, recycle, or trash the following:

- 5 larger toys your child hasn't touched in 6 months
- 10 smaller toys your child hasn't touched in 6 months
- 5 books that your child is too old for
- 3 puzzles, craft kits, or board games that never get played with
- 10 stuffed animals (they really have too many)
- Any broken toys or toys with missing pieces

I can reduce toy clutter in the future by...

My kids would clean up their toys more often if...

Toy Rotation Is like Having Christmas Morning Every Month!

If a straight up purge is too emotionally tough, pack up some toys and rotate what is available and what is in storage every few weeks or months. It is a great way to combat toy clutter and keep children excited about their existing toys.

My children would like toy rotation because...

____

____

____

____

____

____

Some specific toys I could put into a monthly or seasonal rotation are...

____

____

____

____

____

____

____

When it comes to the toys in my home, I feel...

- We have too many
- We have the right amount

Having less toys would be a good thing because...

WARNING

THIS BEDROOM IS CONDEMNED

STEP 17

Declutter Kids' Bedrooms

Kids' bedrooms can be gross, especially if you have teenagers. Stop the madness (and the stink) and tackle your kid's bedroom once and for all.

It's time to embrace minimalism in your child's bedroom. Just like your own bedroom, their room should also be a peaceful and relaxing place to rest and not a stressful, stinky hole to toss their stuff.

Decluttering your child's bedroom will help make it more manageable for them and it will teach them the benefits of not having an overwhelming amount of material possessions.

Decluttering and organization are important life skills that will have a huge impact on their future success. If they are reluctant to let go of unused items—remember, it's your job as their parent to set boundaries and limits on their stuff. Just like you wouldn't let your kids eat cake for breakfast, you also shouldn't let your kids hoard five hundred stuffed animals either.

Stop Growing So Fast!

I can guarantee your child has a lot of clothing in their room that no longer fits them! A lot of it I bet is just lying on the floor. I mean, why can't they just pick up their clothes?!

Take a few minutes to find and recycle/donate/trash the following:

- 5 shirts that no longer fit or are never worn
- 4 pairs of pants that no longer fit or are never worn
- 3 stained, ripped, or faded pieces of clothing
- 4 pairs of underwear that are too small
- 6 pairs of socks they have outgrown (or singles without a match)
- 2 articles of dress clothing that are too small
- 3 pairs of shoes or boots that no longer fit

I haven't taken the time to declutter my child's old clothing because...

____

____

____

____

____

____

____

____

____

Having so much clothing in the bedroom makes life harder because...

I can donate my child's old clothing to...

It's Your Room, But It's My House

You wouldn't let your child eat whatever they want or stay out with friends as long they want. You have rules. Likewise, having rules for your child's bedroom isn't mean, *it's parenting.*

The biggest issue in my child's bedroom is...

____

____

____

____

____

____

____

____

____

Having an organized bedroom would benefit my child because...

____

____

____

____

____

____

____

I can help my child keep their bedroom tidy by (circle all that apply) ...

Getting a Closet Organizer

Under the Bed Storage

Buying Some Baskets

Buying a Shelf

Lighting a Match

Purging Clothing

Selling My Child On Ebay...(Just Kidding)
selling Their Unused Things on Ebay

Getting A Garbage Can

Putting the Laundry Basket in the Middle of the Room

Taking off the Closet Doors

I have so much paperwork, my paperwork has paperwork

STEP 18

Declutter Paper

Most everyone's biggest organizing nemesis is...*paper*. I thought we were becoming a paperless society! Why do we have so much? What do we do with it all? Why does it never. stop. coming?!

Stuffed into drawers or piled to the sky, mail, documents and flyers quickly take over your home. Our first instinct is usually to "just deal with it later," but that is how small piles of paper turn into mountains.

One of the most common reasons we let this happen is out of fear. We are afraid of getting rid of a piece of paper that may be important, so we save absolutely everything. The best way to combat this fear is to know exactly what you need to keep and what you can get rid of.

The great Martha Stewart suggests: "...saving paid utility bills, annual investment statements, and copies of checks for non-tax-deductible items **for one year** (after one year, they can all be shredded). Any IRS tax records, bank statements, and records of deductible expenses should be kept for **up to seven years**. Contracts, home-improvement receipts, mortgage records, and deeds should be kept for **as long as they're active**. Items like marriage papers, education records, and passports **should be kept indefinitely**."

So what do you do with all those electricity bills and bank statements that you've had since 1993? **It's time to shred the suckers!**

It's a Paper Party and Everyone's Invited

If you have a lot of paper, it's time to get the whole family involved! Dedicate a family member to shred anything with your name and personal information on it. Kids are great at this! They love wrecking stuff! Grab a box and fill it with the following papers:

- Bills and statements that are over twelve months old
- Empty envelopes and inserts from old bills
- Old flyers and newspapers
- Old school newsletters
- Old receipts and expired coupons
- Junk mail

We have a lot of paper in our home because...

We can reduce the amount of paper coming in by...

Good Enough Paper System

Stop paper clutter today! Create a system for housing mail, flyers, and school papers right where you already tend to pile it. It doesn't have to be a perfect or complicated system.

Example: Put a simple basket on the counter. Go through and empty it once a week, like on recycling day.

The places we tend to pile our paperwork are...

We can create a system for our incoming paper using...

I can commit to going through my incoming paperwork and filing it every...

Clutter isn't just stuff on your floor, it's anything that stands between you and the life you want to be living.

Peter Walsh

STEP 19

Declutter Garage & Outdoor Space

Do you struggle to scrape your car's windshield each frigid winter morning because there is no room in your garage for your actual car? Do you dream of having a space to work on hobbies and DIY projects, but instead your garage is filled with items your family has outgrown or forgotten about?

If your garage, shed, or outside space is a disaster, you're not alone. These areas are just natural clutter magnets and almost always one of the most neglected areas of a home. They are handy places to stash stuff and so we pile, shove, and stuff our garages or sheds so full of unused junk—they become virtually unusable spaces.

Stop seeing your garage (or shed, etc.) as storage space and start seeing it for all the wonderful things it could be. It's time to make space for new and exciting things to come, and there is no better place to start than in the garage.

What Is This and Why Do I Own It?

Don't want something in your house anymore? Toss it in the garage. This is where unloved items go to die.

Go stand in your garage/shed and take a look around.

Looking around my garage/shed, I see...

I would love to be able to have space in here for...

My dream garage would be used for...

Heave Ho and Away It Goes

Don't wait any longer, it's time to purge!

Here is a helpful checklist of things you can let go of today:

- Boxes that you haven't opened in the past twelve months
- Old bottles of oil, paint, or cleaners
- Gardening equipment you never use
- Sporting equipment you haven't used in the past twelve months
- Tools that are broken or you no longer need
- Seasonal decor that you never put out

If your garage/shed is really full, consider renting a dumpster, filling up a truck to take to the donation center, or having a garage sale to get rid of stuff fast.

I haven't taken the time to declutter my garage/shed because...

____

____

____

____

____

____

____

____

____

____

A clutter-free garage/shed will improve my life because…

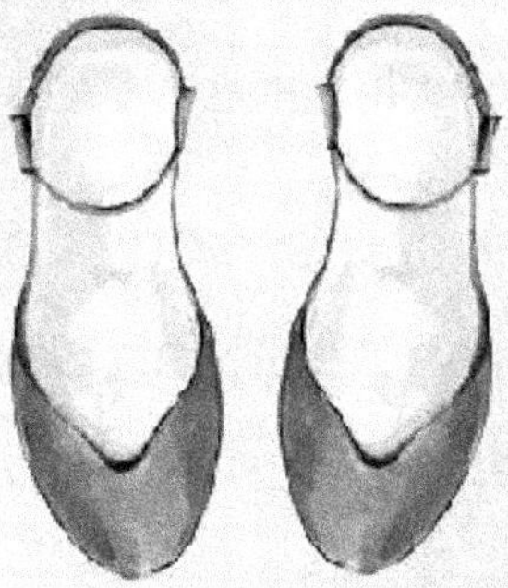

It does not matter how great your shoes are if you don't accomplish anything in them.

-Martina Boone

STEP 20

Declutter Outerwear

If you live in an area with four seasons, you know the struggle of having outerwear for all of the different weather conditions.

Spring jackets, rain jackets, parkas, snow pants, gloves, mittens, hats, and scarves for each family member can add up to a ridiculous amount of outerwear that rarely can be crammed into a typical coat closet efficiently.

Let's not forget about one of the biggest clutter contributors in most homes today: *shoes, boots and sandals*. Why do we have so much footwear?

Even if you are not a shoe lover, it's easy to be overwhelmed with shoe clutter, especially if you have children. Rain boots, winter boots, flip flops, running shoes, dress shoes...it's not unrealistic for each family member to own a minimum of five or six pairs of shoes.

If you come home after a long day, and are overwhelmed by messy piles of shoes, kids' backpacks, and coats the moment you step in the door...you are not alone. In this step, we will tackle the mountains of outerwear to ensure that we are no longer overwhelmed by clutter the minute we open the door. Today is the day your entrance way is transformed into an inviting and organized space, once and for all!

I Just Rescued a Pair of Shoes, They Were Trapped in a Store

Even if you don't think you have a shoe obsession, I guarantee you still own too many pairs.

My current coat and shoe storage make me feel...

When I buy a new pair of shoes, I rarely get rid of an old pair because...

A reasonable number of shoes for myself would be...

Pairs of rubber boots

Pairs of running shoes

Pairs of sandals

Pairs of flip flops

Pairs of dress shoes

Pairs of casual shoes

Pairs of winter boots

Other

Total:

But, I currently own pairs of shoes.

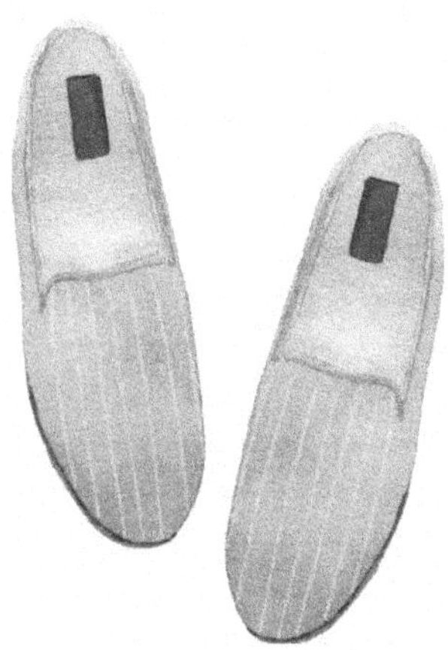

If I Trip Over One More Shoe...

No more tripping over shoes or having to squeeze your coat into a stuffed closet. The mess in your entrance way ends today. Grab a box and donate the following:

- 2 pairs of old shoes for each family member
- 2 pairs of worn out flip flops (you know you have some)
- 1 pair of high heels that kill your feet (no matter how much you paid or how cute they are)
- 1 old coat from each family member
- 6 pairs of gloves, mittens, hats, or scarves that are never worn by anyone
- ALL shoes your children have outgrown

I need to pare down the amount of outerwear in my home because...

____

____

____

____

____

____

____

____

____

____

How will having an organized and clutter-free entrance way make my life easier?

Clutter is the physical manifestation of unmade decisions fueled by procrastination

- Christina Scalise

STEP 21

Declutter Storage Spaces

Do you have the basement blues? Do you struggle with closets that are bursting with random stuff that has no other place to go? Is what's under your bed much scarier than the actual boogie man? Our storage spaces can easily become a generic dumping ground for all things that we just don't want to deal with right now. Cluttered storage is almost always the result of procrastination or indecision. When we don't have time, patience, or any idea what to do with something, we usually stuff it in a closet, basement, or other storage area to deal with "later." But you aren't going to use something more by storing it in a closet.

Let's stop looking at our storage spaces as useless, cluttered black holes and instead see them as potential additional living space for our homes.

Imagine if all the things in your storage area were suddenly gone, what could you use that space for instead? How could you reclaim some extra living space by better utilizing your storage areas?

You could you turn a closet into a mini office space or crafting closet. Perhaps you could move off-season clothing to this now empty closet and free up more space in your bedroom. Maybe that corner or tiny room in your basement could be transformed into a place to work on hobbies, instead of storage for items you *never* use.

How much usable square footage is your unused stuff in storage costing you?

Out with the Old to Make Room for the New

You need to give yourself a dose of tough love. The days of keeping unused things out of guilt or obligation are gone. Today is a fresh start and a new beginning for you.

It's time to let go of...

- Old holiday decor you never use
- Family heirlooms you don't actually like
- Baby clothes or toys your child has outgrown
- Empty boxes...because...why???
- Gifts you have received that you wish you hadn't
- Anything broken...no, you are never going to fix it
- Anything from the '70s, '80s, or '90s that you still have
- Exercise equipment that is just collecting dust
- Old school textbooks or binders

The weirdest thing I found in my storage area was...

____

____

____

____

____

____

____

If I decluttered my storage area I could...

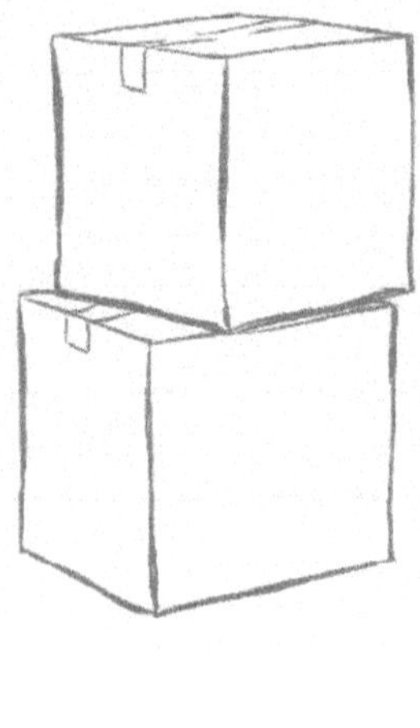

One day, all of your
parents' old random
junk will become yours

STEP 22

Declutter All the Crap That Has No Category

Sometimes when life is crazy, we run on autopilot. Kids come home with some clay sculpture monstrosity, so you just stick it in the corner. Forgot to return those pants that didn't fit? Toss the bag in the bottom of the closet forever. Did the vacuum cleaner break? Buy a new one and just never throw out the old one because...you didn't know where to put it until garbage day.

Today is the day you finally let go of all that random crap hanging around your house because you literally had no idea what else to do with it at the time.

My husband's bedside table has the leaning tower of old electronics on it because he is waiting until he can wipe all the info off before disposing of them. I'm talking about twelve years' worth of old tablets and cell phones, just slowly getting stacked to the sky. I dust them. Every week, I *dust* his tower of electronic clutter.

Maybe, in your case, you worry about the proper way to recycle things such as batteries, medicine, or cleaning supplies. Perhaps you feel awful throwing things away knowing that they will just end up in a landfill somewhere. When you aren't sure how to dispose of something, holding onto it forever shouldn't be your go-to plan. Your home is *not* a viable alternative to a landfill, just sayin'. Believe it or not, there is this super new-fangled thingy that can help you decide how to dispose of your items safely and properly. It'll change your life. It's called *the Google*.

Look around your home and find all that random stuff you have been ignoring and finally take some action. Google where or how to get rid of it. Do it now. I'll wait.

When in Doubt, Throw It Out

Not sure what to do with something? Throw it in the garbage. For reals, it's liberating. (Except for toxic items that should be disposed of properly. In no way do I advocate for earth-killing illegal dumping.)

Here are some things to get started throwing out right now:

- Burned down candles
- Random cords and cables
- Old electronics (like phones, video games, DVD players)
- Broken stuff
- Items you are NEVER going to actually return (Donate these items)
- Greeting cards...seriously, they gotta go
- Cleaning supplies that you don't like
- Old cans of paint
- Gifts from your mother-in-law

I have a hard time letting go of random clutter because...

I need to make myself and my home a priority and stop worrying about the "right" way to declutter or what people may think. The items I'm not sure the "right" thing to do with are...

I can trust myself to make the right decisions for my things because...

Seize the Moment, Because Tomorrow You Might Be Dead

There is nothing worse than the thought of dying and leaving all of our random clutter for someone else to deal with. Swedish Death Cleaning is a real thing, and we all need to jump on this bandwagon.

If I dropped dead tomorrow, I wouldn't want my loved ones to have to deal with...

If my home burned down tomorrow, the only things I would really miss are...

I'm committed to keeping my home clutter-free because...

You're not messy,
you just organize
differently

- Clutterbug -

STEP 23

What's Your Organizing Style?

Now that you are a decluttering boss, it's time to do a little organization. Organizing is about creating homes for all of your stuff, so it's easier to put things away and find those things again when you need them.

Organizing isn't one size-fits-all, so before you create homes for your belongings, it's helpful to understand your unique organizing style.

There are visual organizers, who like to have their everyday items out in the open where they can see them. Visual organizers often struggle with "out of sight, out of mind" so they subconsciously leave their things out, so they don't forget about them. Having everything hidden behind closed doors causes anxiety in a visual organizer.

The opposite, of course, are hidden organizers. They prefer to store their items out of sight in order to have their home feel visually simplified. This type of organizer is more traditional in the sense that they prefer all of their items in drawers, cabinets, and behind closed doors. A lot of visual stimulation triggers their anxiety, so their everyday items are hidden away.

Of course this is a sliding scale, but I want you to picture a space in your home that stays pretty organized, without much effort. Is this space visual or hidden? **Do you relate more to the visual or the hidden organizer?**

Now let's break down the other half of the organizing styles. Some people are **detail oriented**. I call these **"micro organizers"** because they prefer to sort their items into smaller categories and their brain naturally thinks in terms of complex plans and fine details.

The opposite are people who are more **"big picture"** kind of thinkers. I call these **"macro organizers"** because they prefer larger, less detailed categories for fast and easy use.

Micro organizers prefer to find their items quickly and don't mind taking a few seconds to put things away properly.

Macro organizers prefer to put away their items quickly and don't mind taking a few seconds to find the exact item they need.

Do you relate more to the "micro" or "macro" style of organizing?

ladybug
cricket
butterfly
bee

What Clutterbug Are You?

If you are a visual and macro organizer, you are a Butterfly.

If you are a hidden and macro organizer, you are a Ladybug.

If you are a visual and micro organizer, you are a Bee.

If you are a hidden and micro organizer, you are a Cricket.

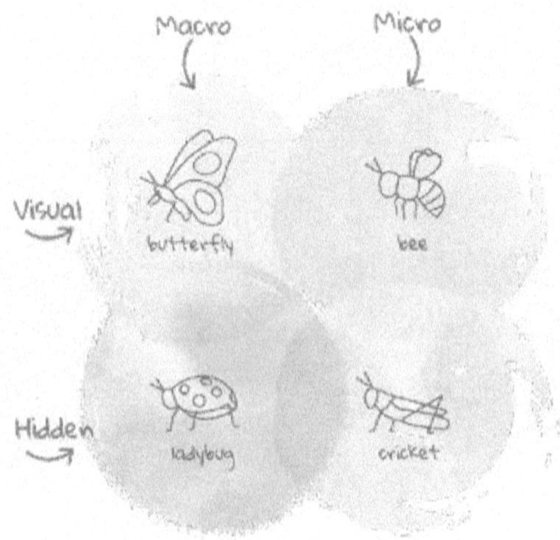

I think I am a __________ because...

___

___

___

___

___

___

___

___

For more information on your Clutterbug style, visit www.clutterbug.com.

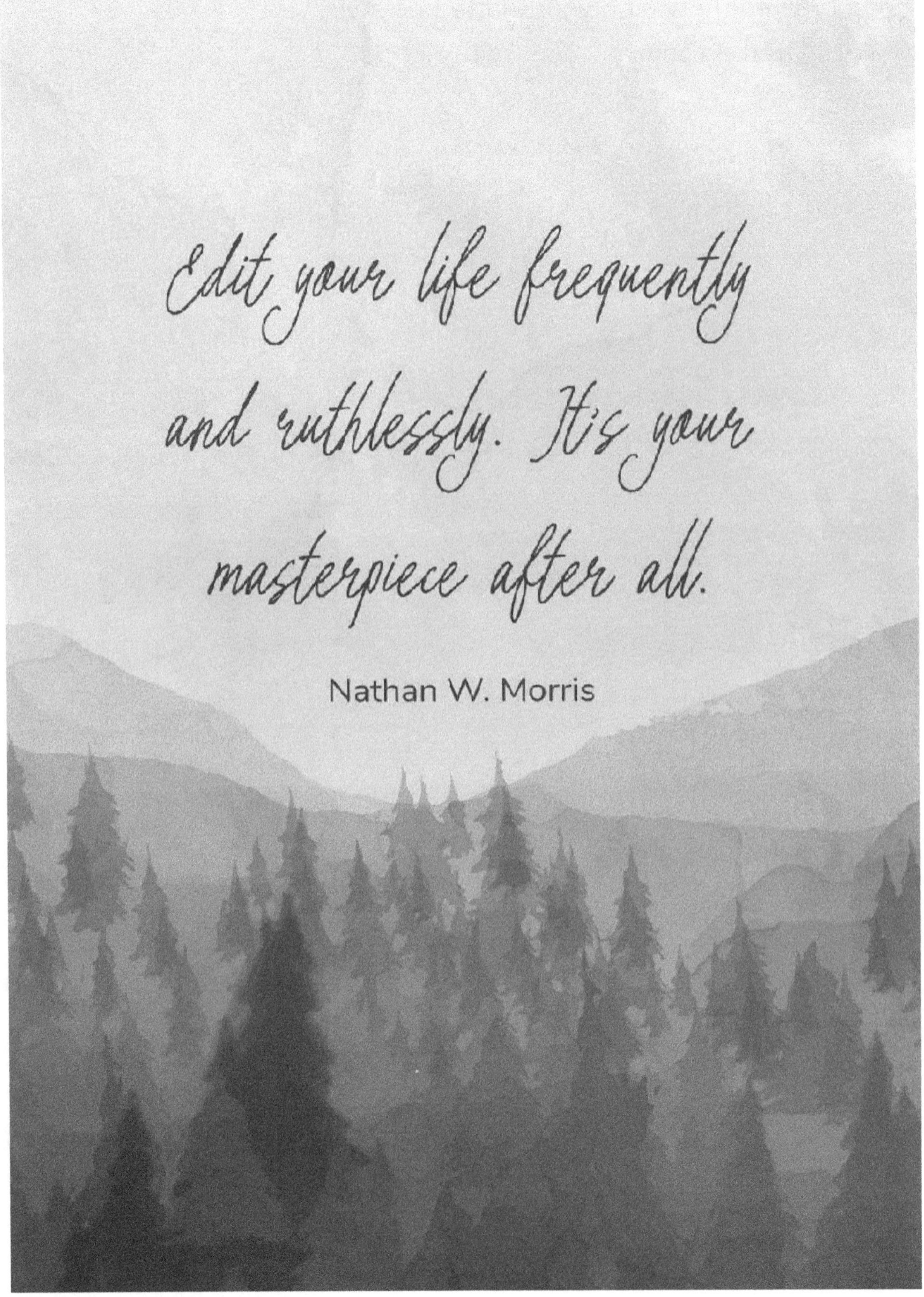
Edit your life frequently
and ruthlessly. It's your
masterpiece after all.
Nathan W. Morris

STEP 24

Organizing Must Haves

Now that you know what type of Clutterbug you are, it will be easier to create organizing systems that compliment your style.

There are a few key areas of your home that are going to require some ongoing organizing maintenance in order to stay clutter-free. For obvious reasons, the high traffic areas usually become dumping grounds for the most clutter. Focus on creating simple solutions to catch clutter where it starts, to stop it from spreading to the rest of your home.

Landing Zone – As soon as you enter you home, you need to have a dedicated spot for keys, wallets, coats, shoes, backpacks...all the stuff that usually gets dropped on the floor or piled on your flat surfaces. A landing zone can be as simple as some hooks (for visual organizers) or a small cabinet (for hidden organizers) right at your front door.

Action File – Every home needs a place to drop the mail, kids schoolwork, and other papers that you bring home. An action file is a place that your "I have to deal with this" paper lives until you have a chance to actually deal with it. This can be as simple as hanging a paper sorter on the wall or placing a basket on your kitchen counter to catch all your incoming paper.

Household Management Binder – There will always be random papers we need for our home and a binder is the perfect place to store these.

In my binder, I could keep:

- Kids school information
- Medical information
- Emergency contacts
- Family mailing lists
- Cleaning checklists
- Pet information
- Business cards from contractors
- Take out menus
- Coupons

Donation Bin – Now that you are a decluttering boss, I recommend keeping a bin or box in your home where you toss items that you no longer need, whenever you come across them. I have a bin in the bottom of each family member's closet for clothing that is too small or we no longer wear. This helps regular decluttering become an easy habit! Just don't forget to periodically empty the bin!

Your Organizing Plan

Areas that are already organized

Areas I need to work on

Things I want to organize first...

Supplies I need

A home for everything and

everything in its home

STEP 25

Surface Clutter Challenge

Having a plan for your home's clutter hot spots will help you stop the creep of clutter from coming back. Think about those surfaces that seem to attract clutter like a magnet, no matter how often you tidy them up. The top of dressers, tables, and kitchen counters are usually the biggest offenders.

I challenge you to start a daily routine to tackle surface clutter, so that it never gets out of control again. A quick five-minute "tidy time" is all you need to clear your surface clutter each night before bed. I recommend using a bin for "homeless clutter" where you can drop those "I have no freaking idea what to do with this right now stuff" into for fast and easy decluttering. Again, just don't forget to periodically empty this bin.

Clear out the clutter and
you just might find that it
was blocking the door
you were looking for

Katrina Mayer

My Daily Declutter Plan

Identify a few areas of your home where you will commit to doing a daily, “quick five-minute tidy up” routine.

Every day I will spend five minutes tidying...

- The kitchen
- The entryway
- The bathroom
- ____________________
- ____________________
- ____________________
- ____________________

The one space that gets the messiest the fastest is...

Cleaning and organizing is a

PRACTICE

not a project

Meagan Francis

STEP 26

You Are the Queen of Clean

Hands up if you love to clean!

Yeah, I didn't think there would be many of us. Granted, cleaning the house isn't exactly the most fun thing to do, but it's an important part of adulting. No one likes living in a messy, dirty home.

In this step, we will work on identifying what will best motivate you to clean! There are many ways to make housework more enjoyable, and... spoiler alert, it has a lot to do with your mindset (are you groaning?).

Changing your mindset will help you realize that the benefits of a clean home outweigh the struggle of actually having to clean it. It's about adding a few small, daily routines into your life so that eventually, cleaning is something you do without even realizing you are doing it. Most importantly, it's about understanding that cleaning your home isn't a chore. It's a gift to yourself.

So grab your favorite cleaning product and let's go scrub some $#!&!

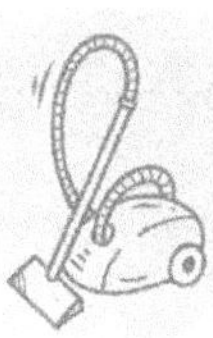

I had to clean my house for two hours just to tell guests

"SORRY ABOUT THE MESS!"

Your Belief about Housework

Thinking of housework as a never-ending chore that no one appreciates is all wrong. YOU are the one who loves and appreciates having a clean home. You aren't cleaning for or because of someone else, you're doing it for you because you deserve it.

I procrastinate cleaning my home because...

I love having a clean home because...

Circle all the ways cleaning your home is a positive thing.

A clean home motivates me

A clean home is healthier

I can entertain guests

A clean house makes me happy

Cleaning is relaxing

I feel proud when it's clean

I'm not embarrassed by my home

A clean house is less stressful

My home looks better

A clean house smells nice

Decluttering isn't
a chore, it's a
gift to yourself.

- Clutterbug -

Motivational Cleaning Mindset

You have the power to make cleaning more enjoyable and yes, it's all in how you look at it. Try pairing it with something fun so that you are both motivated and feeling positive about getting to clean!

Some positive things I can do while cleaning are:

- Listen to music
- Listen to an audiobook
- Listen to a podcast
- Watch a YouTube cleaning video (this really works)
- Talk to a friend on the phone as you work
- Set a timer for fifteen minutes and see how much you can get done, or make it a contest between family members
- Invite a friend or family member to help, then help them with their place
- ____________________
- ____________________
- ____________________

When all else fails, invite your mother-in-law over! Nothing gets me motivated to clean like when company's coming.

Changing my thoughts about housework will help motivate me because...

____

____

____

Cleaning Routines

A quick daily cleaning routine means you are no longer a slave to housework on the weekends. Doing a little bit every day is the secret to having a home that never really gets too dirty in the first place. Go ahead and add a few tasks to this sample daily routine:

- Make your bed
- Do the dishes
- Wipe down kitchen counters
- Wipe down the bathroom
- Do a five-minute tidy up
- Spot mop spills or crumbs on floors
- Put away clothes and shoes
- ______________________
- ______________________
- ______________________
- ______________________

How long do you think this list will take you to complete? Why not test it? Set a timer and see!

I think this list will take me...

____

This list actually took me...

____

If I do this every day, I will get faster at it because...

YOU can't force someone else to Change

BUT YOU CAN CHANGE YOUR OWN

ATTITUDE & EXPECTATIONS

STEP 27

Get Your Family on Board

I can't tell you how many times I've heard people complain that their spouse doesn't help clean or tidy the house. It is frustrating to feel like all of the household responsibilities are on your shoulders and it's easy to feel disappointed when your family doesn't rise to meet the expectations you have for them. Household resentment in relationships is a freaking epidemic, but I do have a cure. No, I can't force your spouse and children to start picking up after themselves, but I can help you manage your expectations and attitude. This makes a huge difference, and when *you* are coming from a place of positivity, I promise you'll find that your family will help more.

People avoid tasks that they think they suck at. This is why nagging your spouse or children to clean or, calling them "lazy" or "messy" never makes the situation better. If someone associates housework with failure (including failure to meet your standards when they do try), they aren't exactly going to be motivated to do it more often.

I know what you may be thinking, *If they just picked up after themselves, I'd stop being angry* or *I just want them to be respectful of me and my time*. I understand how you feel; but this isn't about you. People are not "messy" just to upset someone else and they certainly won't start changing their behavior because they are being nagged or yelled at. **People change behaviors and habits because that change makes them feel good about themselves.**

In this step, we will focus on how you can change your thoughts and attitude about housework in order to encourage your family to follow your lead. It will be about letting go of control and changing expectations as well as using positive reinforcement to get them to clean up after themselves. Am I suggesting that you fake a little extra niceness, even when they don't deserve it? Yes, yes, I am. Changing your mindset is going to be really hard work, but I promise it will be worth it.

Judge Your Spouse

This incredible exercise was created by Byron Katie. I have slightly modified it here to specifically fit "household chore resentment." I've worked on many of my own issues using Byron Katie's worksheets and I have to say, it's been a life-changing transformation.

1. When it comes to housework, who most upsets and disappoints you and why? I am feeling ____________ (emotion) with ____________ (name) because__________________________.
2. When it comes to housework, how or what do you want him/her to change? I want ________________ (name) to ____.
3. What advice would you give to him/her? ___________ (name) should/shouldn't ____.
4. In order for you to be happy, what do you need them to say, think, or do differently? I need _____________ (name) to ____.
5. Make a list of how you feel about their homemaking skills. It's ok to be petty.)

   ____

   ____

   ____

   ____

   ____
6. What is something that you never want him/her to do again? I don't ever want ________________ (name) to ___________________________________.

The Flip Side

Now it's time to flip your answers around and see if perhaps your perception and expectations are making the situation worse.

Reread question number 1 from the last exercise, but this time list 3 ways that the person who upsets you most DOESN'T always do the things you listed. Example: If you wrote "I am angry at Joe because he never helps with housework." You will instead write: "My statement isn't true because he loads the dishwasher, does the laundry, and does yard work."

My statement isn't always true because...

____

____

____

____

____

____

____

____

____

Reread question number 2, 3, 4 and 5, and this time reread each statement, replacing the person's name with "I" or "me." Example: Instead of saying: "I want Joe to pick up after himself more often" change this to "I want me to pick up more often". How did that make you feel? Where any of those statements about yourself true?

How did that make you feel? Where any of those statements about yourself true?

When I turned my statements around on myself, I felt...

____

____

____

____

____

____

____

____

Rereading question number 6, what would happen if you reacted differently to the thing that he/she does that you wish they wouldn't? Could the things that they do present an opportunity for you to start an honest conversation or work on a more positive mindset? Instead change "I don't ever want" to "I look forward to."

Example: "I don't ever want Joe to leave his dirty dishes on the counter again". Instead I could say: "I look forward to when Joe leaves his dirty dishes on the counter again because it will give me a chance to talk to him about how I sometimes feel disrespected."

When he/she does these things I feel/react this way...

____

____

____

Instead of getting upset, things would be different if I...

When I changed my statement from "I don't ever want" to "I look forward to " I realize that this person's behavior may be a good opportunity for me to...

The Stick or the Carrot

The carrot or the stick metaphor refers to an old story about getting a donkey to pull a heavy cart. You can either dangle a carrot in front of him or hit him in the behind with a stick. In my experience, "carrots" work much better when you want to motivate someone to start a new habit or behavior. That, and I don't recommend hitting your family members with a stick.

In the past, I have tried to get my family to clean by...

____

____

____

____

____

____

Instead of complaining or nagging, wait until someone shows initiative (however small) and praise them for it. Did your daughter pick her wet towel off the bathroom floor without being asked? Acknowledge this behavior. Thank her and let her know how happy it made you.

List some other ways you can use positive reinforcement to trick...er... motivate your family into being helpful around the house.

I can try to be more positive to my family when they...

____

____

____

If CLARITY

is what you want,

Being Focused

will get you there.

STEP 28

Clarity and Focus for Your Home

Your goals for your home should now be crystal clear. You want a clean, clutter-free, and organized home. Your underlying reason for those goals should also be clear. You want a home that is stress-free, inviting, and easy to maintain.

You finally have CLARITY, and that is awesome; but how do you stay focused on those goals over the long term? Willpower and hard work are not enough to achieve long-lasting success and happiness. The real key is your *emotions*.

Maintaining clarity and focus is all about pinpointing the feeling that achieving your goals will manifest. Outcomes are awesome, but it's our *emotions* that truly motivate us.

In this step, we are going to determine what *really* motivates you by discovering how you want your home to make you *feel* about yourself. Every concrete goal we make is really about wanting to *feel* a certain way about ourselves when we achieve it. When we can identify that feeling and shift our focus to that emotion being our real end goal, that is how we can achieve real and long-lasting motivation and happiness.

Let's Get Touchy Feely

Close your eyes and imagine coming home to your dream home. Visualize it. What does it *feel* like?

I want my home to feel...

How do you want your goal to make you feel about yourself?

I want to feel...

What can you do OTHER than cleaning and organizing your home to feel this way about yourself?

I can feel this way about myself by...

REAL TALK: YOU DON'T NEED TO DO ANYTHING IN ORDER TO FEEL THIS WAY ABOUT YOURSELF. YOU CAN CHOOSE TO FEEL THIS WAY ABOUT YOURSELF RIGHT NOW.

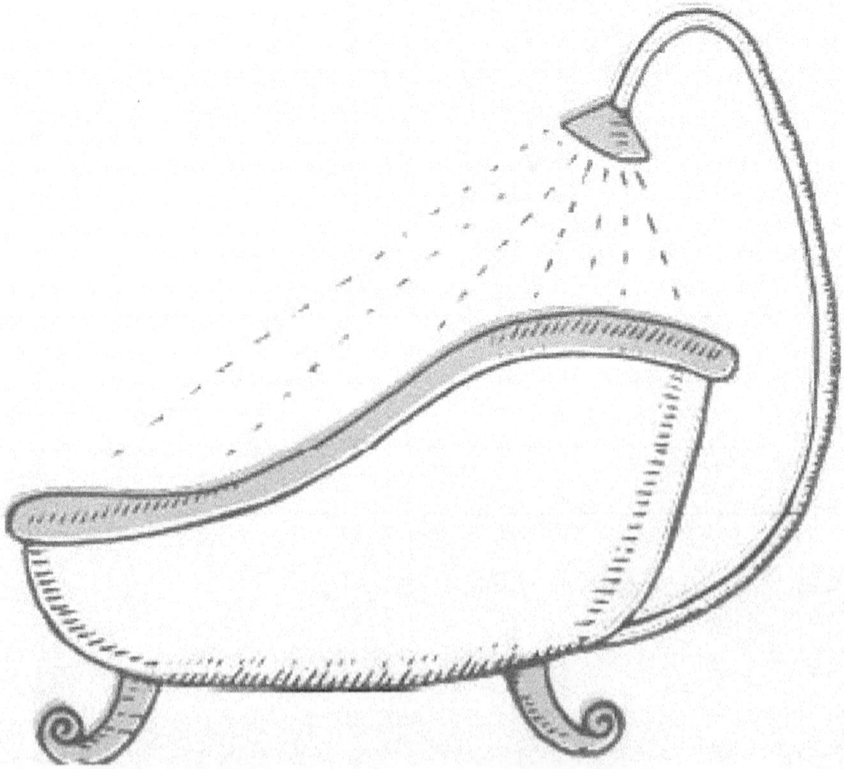

IT'S OK TO BE

PROUD OF YOURSELF

STEP 29

Moving Forward

You've accomplished **so much** with this journal, but decluttering is an ongoing process. You'll never be completely finished, and that is ok because your home is a journey, not a destination. Focus on how far you've come, not on how far you have left to go. Congratulate yourself on all your success up to this point.

Through this journey you've learned so much about yourself, you've changed your mindset and became more a more positive person, and hopefully you are being much kinder to yourself. Be proud of everything you have achieved and how much clutter you have let go of so far.

New Day, New You

Look around at your space and ask yourself; "Does my home reflect who I am today?" Example: Old me loved African art, new me likes a more cottage feel. Old me loved Stephen King novels, new me loves reading self-help books.

Old You	**New You**

Look at your list and then take a look around at your space. It's time to let go of anything that isn't supporting the *you* that you are today.

What is the one accomplishment you reached on this journey that you are the proudest of?

I am most proud of myself for...

The Sky's the Limit

Take a few minutes to brain dump all the future goals you have for yourself, even if they are not related to your home in anyway. You are amazing and you can accomplish anything and everything you want from life.

If you're brave enough
to say goodbye, life will
reward you with a
new hello.
- Paulo Coelho

STEP 30

Parting Is Such Sweet Sorrow

The time has come to say goodbye to this journal.

You don't need it anymore. You've come so far, and you are more than capable of continuing on your decluttering journey without any guides or checklists as guidance. To prove to yourself that you are a decluttering boss, I want you to declutter this journal *right now*. Trash it, recycle it, bury it, burn it...I don't care, just as long as it leaves your home. Before you go, however, reflect on the following:

This decluttering journey has made me feel...

I've discovered so much about myself, including...

A Note from the Author

Thank you so much for allowing me to be a small part of your decluttering journey. I hope that within these pages you have discovered a little more love for your home and a lot more love for yourself. I hope you feel inspired and motivated to continue this journey on your own. More than anything though, I hope decluttering has made your life easier and happier, because you really do deserve it.

OK, NOW REALLY GET RID OF THIS THING RIGHT NOW.

CPSIA information can be obtained
at www.ICGtesting.com
Printed in the USA
LVHW061736090422
715792LV00009B/492

9 781803 340425